# SALUTE

# SALUTE

A Military Wife's Poetic Allegiance to

Faith, Family, and Friends

★ PATTI A. TUCKER ★

WinePressPublishing
Great Books, Defined.

WinePress Publishing is honored to present this title in partnership with the author. The views expressed or implied in this work are those of the author. WinePress provides our imprint seal representing design excellence, creative content and high quality production. To learn more about Responsible Publishing™ visit www.winepresspublishing.com.

**Hard Cover:**
ISBN 13: 978-1-4141-2493-3
ISBN 10: 1-4141-2493-7

**Soft Cover:**
ISBN 13: 978-1-4141-2492-6
ISBN 10: 1-4141-2492-9

Library of Congress Catalog Card Number: 2012918089

# DEDICATION

I want to express my heartfelt thanks to my husband, Terry, for his encouragement and collaboration in putting this book together. Thank you for your faithfulness and love in allowing me to follow my dreams and for supporting me in this endeavor.

Our journey through the military for nearly thirty-four years taught me many things: the value of trusting in God, family is everything, and inspiration comes from true friends.

# CONTENTS

## Section 4: Friendship Is Forever

## Section 5: Military Assignments and Families

## Section 6: My Favorite Holidays

## Section 7: Elvis the King

# FOREWORD

*Salute—A poetic allegiance to faith, family, and friends* is a collection of moving and personal memories of a military spouse about her faith, family, and life as an Army wife and the many friends she made along the way.

The author has spent a lifetime balancing God, family, and friends. Known for caring for and giving to others before self, her writings exemplify that genuine caring and down-to-earth approach in all things. This collection is heartwarming and expresses the values of a true patriotic American woman.

—**Terry L. Tucker**
Major General (Retired)
Loving Husband

# Section 1
# MY FAMILY

# REFLECTIONS

Who is this reflection I now see,
This woman who is changing and growing in me?

Many roles I have been commissioned with and blest,
Daughter, wife, mother, grandmother, and friend,
all given my best.

These places I have journeyed and people I have met
Have brought me to this moment now I cannot forget.

A reflection that now shows signs of age,
But one that reveals wisdom and lights a new page.

A page in my life that I now can embrace
By a power above who has given me grace.

Reflections that reveal in a small part
Some special memories instilled in my heart.

Terry and I had a beautiful wedding at our home church
in Dunbar, West Virginia. We were both so young.
We have now spent over forty-two years
together as best friends.

# FOREVER LOVE

A forever love is you and me,
One that was meant to always be.
Love at first sight it seemed,
Constantly present in my dreams.

Starting out just as kids we were,
Learning to rely on each other for sure.
Entering the military became our life,
Wherever we traveled, I was a devoted wife.

While in Germany we had a boy,
Who filled our life with much joy.
Traveling all around the world,
Washington State would bring us our baby girl.

Then in a year of turmoil called Desert Storm,
You would lead your soldiers bravely to perform.
Now thirty-three years together,
Our forever love is as strong as ever.

A forever love is you and me,
One that was meant to always be.
Days of happiness and sadness we have seen,
But our forever love will forever beam.

"A Tribute to my Mom" was written in dedication to my dear Mother
prior to her death in 2001.
It is an expression
of my eternal love to an angel of a Mom who
sacrificed everything for me.

# A TRIBUTE TO MY MOM

Always there when I was small,
Ready to catch me if I should fall.

Patching up a cut or skinned knee,
She immediately came to rescue me.

Often calming my nerves and fears,
Standing by to gently wipe my tears.

Instilling moral values and sound advice,
Going without often to sacrifice.

Demonstrating the warmth of kindness and generosity,
Teaching me how to share the feeling of hospitality.

Countless ways she showed me love,
Is a priceless gift from heaven above.

A guardian angel, confidante, and best friend,
She was always there to lend a helping hand.

I alone was lucky as no other
To be blessed to call her Mother.

Dad enlisted in the Navy during World War II and
served aboard the USS *Ira Jeffery.*
Although he could be a stubborn and very independent man,
he had undying love for me that never faltered.

# INVINCIBLE

This man who seemed invincible,
Held his head high on stubborn principles.
A Dad who sometimes was testy and stern,
But always came through with genuine concern.

During the time of the Great Depression he would struggle to
survive,
Overcoming trials and obstacles with persevering drive.
A Navy man who served in the Pacific,
Proudly wore the uniform and looked terrific.

An occupation of electronics would be his call,
Repairing and fine tuning he dedicated his all.
After losing his beloved wife,
He somehow lost his desire for life.

I will always remember his invincible ways,
And miss and love him the rest of my days.

No mother could be more proud of a son. Christopher,
a scholar, combat veteran Marine,
and successful businessman, has been all I could ask for.

# A MOTHER'S PRIDE

Seen in the eyes is a mother's pride
At the arrival of a son, her love she can't hide.

Born in a small German town,
He could always turn a frown upside down.

Possessing musical talents and a gift of voice,
Hobbies of scouts, track, and guitar would be his choice.

As the high school days soon wound down,
An interest in soldiering soon was found.

In the Marines he would deploy to Iraq,
Leading a battalion and bringing all his unit's men safely
back.

Now owning a title company has become his occupation,
Managing to help and serve his town with selfless dedication.

A mother's pride can still be seen
In her adult son who has fulfilled her every dream.

Tracey '98

Bonds between mothers and daughters are like no other.
I am so proud of what Tracey has done:
great teacher, dedicated wife, wonderful mother,
and caring humanitarian.

# A CHERISHED GIFT

A cherished gift is what you are,
More precious than any twinkling star.

A wintry January day in Washington State,
Was a joyous and eventful date.

As a toddler you were so cute and sweet,
Adorable as any child you could ever meet.

Playing the saxophone and cheering on the squad,
An energetic teen whom I always would applaud.

Now all grown with talent to teach,
You will inspire and challenge all you reach.

A cherished gift that can never be replaced
Is found in the beauty of my daughter's face.

In October 2007, Tracey and Chris Kreuzer were wed and
joined their "Two Hearts."
I am delighted she found the love of her life.

# TWO HEARTS

Two hearts will be joined today,
May the love they share never stray.

The rings exchanged as a special token
Will justify the sacred vows spoken.

The hope of a future filled with bliss
Will be lovingly sealed with a kiss.

Promising to honor until death,
Ensuring this covenant with committed breath.

Two hearts, may they always be blessed
To live in harmony and receive life's very best.

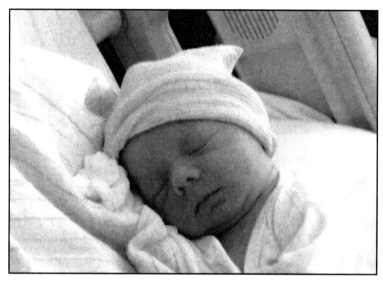

Ethan Michael, born in 2009, is my first grandchild.
Like all grandparents, I know there is no other
like the first grandchild.

# AWAITING A MIRACLE

Awaiting a miracle we now anticipate
With excitement and gladness, a new life to celebrate.

An expectation of a wonderful new baby boy
Will bring much happiness and an abundance of joy.

Ethan Michael will be his chosen name,
And every relative will undoubtedly stake their claim.

Doting parents will burst with pride,
Beaming with emotion they can hardly hide.

Awaiting a miracle soon no longer will be a dream,
But a gift from above which will forever
be held in high esteem.

God has blessed me with two wonderful and healthy
grandchildren. Cooper James is that "new angel"
who made our family complete.

# A NEW ANGEL

A new angel will descend upon earth
In the form of a new baby boy's birth.

Much excitement and joy will be felt
When Cooper James makes hearts melt.

A sweet bundle sent from above
Will fill his home with endless love.

A new angel now who has arrived
Has brought his family so much pride.

An angel with light brown hair who rarely cries
Is quite a miracle in his big brother's eyes.

A new angel will bring happiness and pleasure
And is God's gift to cherish and forever treasure.

Kathleen (Kat) Hunt Moore in a photo taken during
World War II, shortly before marrying Ralph.
"My Favorite Aunt" was written in her honor.
She was always a part of my early years and
was a shining example of a committed Christian woman.

# MY FAVORITE AUNT

She always just calls me Pat,
This favorite aunt, we simply call Kat.
Her special gift of gab she shares with me
And wears a smile for all to see.

Memories of long ago often come to mind when
I was a little girl and she ran to watch me pantomime.
Kindness and patience are her enduring strengths
That have touched so many to great lengths.

A close relationship with our God above
Shows every day in her gifts of love.
For over fifty years she has shared life with her special mate,
And her son and family have brought happiness
for her to celebrate.

She always just calls me Pat,
This favorite aunt, we simply call Kat.
No other aunt could be more important to me
Than my favorite and only aunt whom I'll love eternally.

19

Ralph Moore was a strong presence in my childhood.
His values and faith in God have always been unwavering.

# A SPECIAL MAN

A special man we remember well,
Always sharing stories he loved to tell.

Serving as a mechanic in the Third Armored Division,
He would earn several Victory Medals due to his precision.

Later bus mechanics would be his trade,
Working many long hours at Charleston Transit he stayed.

For sixty-five years he shared life with his faithful mate,
And their bond produced a son they would celebrate.

This special man's legacy as husband, father,
and grandfather will forever be,
Held closely in my heart as he was known as
Uncle Ralph to me.

Rusty is a special dog that most humans can't compare to.
The devotion and love shown to us through
our pets is truly unconditional.

# RUSTY

A special companion that could never be replaced,
The wag of a tail and a sweet lick on the face.

A personality of sweet adoration and loyalty,
Always gives me a feeling of royalty.

A desire to protect and stay constantly by my side,
No human friend could show such pride.

Keeping a watch every day and at dark,
Alerting me, his job is complete with a bark.

No other friend compares to my pet Rusty,
Who demonstrates love and affection and is always trusty.

"The Final Salute" is written for my loving husband
on the completion of our thirty-four year military career.
It was written to honor his dedicated service and
love for our country and the time we spent
serving military families together.

# THE FINAL SALUTE

The final salute we will pay today,
On the occasion of our retirement day.
A Saber, Tank, and Stetson will begin to fade,
These occupational symbols of a tanker's trade.

Allons, Garry Owen, and Tropic Lightning, all mottos proud,
Just a few of the elite we once shouted loud.
Familiar sounds of bugler's call of reveille and retreat,
Will always be sounds so dear and so sweet.

A starched uniform will be put away,
And a pair of spit-shined boots no longer needed today.
Taking care of soldiers and families our best we did try,
Now we must leave them behind and say goodbye.

The final salute we will pay today,
On the occasion of our retirement day.
Such pride no other career could reflect,
Our Army of One and the flag we respect.

# Section 2
# PATRIOTISM

# TERRIBLE TUESDAY

911 was the call and the date,
When so many lives met their fate.

Who would have thought such a crime
Could have happened here in our time?

The World Trade Center hit by hijacked planes
And a part of the pentagon zapped in vain.

A downed plane headed by evil foes,
Averted targets by brave everyday heroes.

Police and firefighters working around the clock,
Trying to rescue and help, dealing with shock.

Sights too horrific to comprehend,
But eyes still focused until the end.

Freedom will ever be a part of this story,
As American hearts are bonded by Old Glory.

May God protect our land from terrorism,
And keep the American spirit alive with patriotism.

Terrible Tuesday will remain heavy in our hearts,
But the spirit of liberty can never depart.

# PATRIOTIC PRIDE

Patriotic pride is the feeling Americans possess,
Living in the best country God chose to bless.

With much bloodshed, sacrifice, and toil,
Countless men fought bravely to protect our precious soil.

Parades, barbecues, and flags waving proudly,
Are symbols of freedom we celebrate wildly.

A gala display of fireworks that light up the sky,
Always bring a shock of awe to our eyes.

Hopefully, we all will forever embrace and not hide,
Our love for God, country, and our patriotic pride.

# RIGHT OF FREEDOM

A right of freedom we should voice
When it comes to deciding our favorite choice.
In early November please make a note
To go to the polls and cast your vote.

No matter your party affiliation,
Take time to make your decision.
In early November please make a note
To go to the polls and cast your vote.

Casting a ballot in this election
Insures your candidate moves in the right direction.
In early November please make a note
To go to the polls and cast your vote.

This right of freedom with which we are blessed,
Is found in our country, the very best.
In early November please make a note
To go to the polls and cast your vote.

Section 3

# SPIRITUAL HEALING

"Enjoying Every Day Because of Joyce"
is dedicated to Joyce Meyer,
one of the world's leading Bible teachers and authors.
Her inspirational word plays a major role in my life
and my closer walk with God.

# ENJOYING EVERY DAY
# BECAUSE OF JOYCE

Enjoying every day because of Joyce allowing me to discover,
What is really important in life and helping me recover.
Dealing with losses and questions I found hard to understand,
Following her program daily, I began to adopt a new plan.

The plan that she explained each day,
Was simply to follow the Word and pray.
Now daily I listen and earnestly continue to pray,
Realizing blessings that have begun to come my way.

Relating to her down-to-earth honesty and humor,
Made it easy to believe and dispute false rumors.
Knowing the depth of pain and abuse
that she has risen above,
Demonstrates her relentless faith and abundance of love.

Enjoying every day because of Joyce allowing me to discover,
What is really important in life and helping me recover.
Each day I will continue to study and earnestly pray,
Enjoying everyday life because Joyce showed me the way.

# GOD'S WAKE-UP CALL

A wake-up call has been made,
To remind the world of God's Word we can't evade.

Wars, rumor of wars, and people turning cold,
All prophecies from the Good Book we must now behold.

A great earthquake, tsunami, and nuclear threat
have been felt,
An unproportional magnitude of disaster has been dealt.

Much human suffering and great heartaches abound,
As an inhumane leader continues his rule and
can't be brought down.

Everywhere visible so much uprising and unrest,
As many nations are facing catastrophe in the
depths of protest.

God's wake-up call is a plea to restore order and peace,
By showing love and kindness and ensuring
that evil must cease.

# STORMS

Storms come into our life and can cause pain,
Rolling, windy, battering events that produce strain.

Dealing with these clouds that we all face,
We often struggle and search for a hiding place.

Although the clear choice is to call on the Lord above,
Most of the world doesn't know His perfect love.

The lightning can strike with a sudden force,
Bringing a rush of fear and take us off course.

Storms not only can be related to weather,
But life's valleys that we often face together.

# WOUNDED WORLD

A wounded world is one in which we now live,
Where people are cold and refuse to give.
No time to look around and see the need,
From so much suffering and too much greed,

Loneliness, illness, and abuse are widespread,
So much poverty where people beg to be fed.
We must take a stand to help wherever we can,
Any small task to help our fellow man.

A wounded world is one in which we now live,
Where people are cold and refuse to give.
Look to our heavenly Father for guidance and direction,
He will show us the way to complete the provision.

# FOR SUCH A TIME

For such a time God has provided a space
That we should be in this moment and place.

A time to help and fulfill needs
For spiritual healing and sowing of productive seeds.

A call to serve and show mercy and grace
In a world filled with hatred and distaste.

A spiritual tugging at our hearts and souls
To reach out and show compassion as our ultimate goal.

For such a time we have been allowed to stay the course,
Not to waste but to be God's driving force.

# DID YOU KNOW?

Did you know that Jesus paid it all?
Did you know that He always will call?

A decision that we all must make,
One we need to address and not forsake.

A tugging on our hearts that we can't deny,
When we surrender everything and release a cry.

Did you know the wonderful promise you will receive,
If you acknowledge Him as Savior and believe?

Did you know that Jesus pleads for us not to hesitate?
Did you know that the time is now and you can't wait?

# POWER OF PRAYER

The power of prayer is an awesome experience.
It can make supernatural things happen, not just coincidence.

Whenever there are more than two gathered to pray,
A holy presence can be felt in the words we say.

A blind man can finally see and a lame man can walk,
If the faith within is more than just talk.

A petition sent to our holy Father will be heard,
And will be answered when we obey His holy Word.

The power of prayer is not just for some,
But for all who enter God's rest and come.

# CHANGE

A need for transition or to rearrange,
Is the result of what transpires when there is change.

Sometimes it seems hard or beyond imagination,
But if divinely directed it can yield a restoration.

Not all change is centered on peace and righteousness,
It can be rooted in anger and bitterness.

Reasoning with the effects of everyday change,
Can be difficult to accept and perceived as strange.

Change can happen in an instant and have
an impact on our life,
But if we focus on God's plan, we can embrace
change and not live with strife.

# ANGELS

Angels are all around, even though not visible to the eye,
They can be our guardians and lift us on high.

These messengers of God can likely come in human form,
Guiding us and protecting us from any turbulent storm.

Beings that likely don't have wings,
But ever so special they can make us sing.

The power that these precious few can possess,
Is an overwhelming force that fills us with bliss.

Angels are those who can bring us peace,
Unique spirits that only heaven could release.

Angels will forever provide strength and hope,
In times of trial will allow us to cope.

# ONE VOICE

When we are called by one clear voice,
We need to take a definitive stand of choice.

Not always easy to know which path is pure,
But with a stirring of our hearts we can be sure.

Being certain that God shines a bright light
To guide us in a world that clouds our sight.

One voice that speaks in a calm, direct way,
Which insures we can't be led astray.

One voice can only be heard
By believers who pray and read the Word.

# HEAVEN

Heaven is a divine place God has obtained for all,
If we will trust Him as our Savior and answer His call.

No more pain, suffering, or tears,
When we are delivered from all our fears.

Pearly gates and streets of gold,
Is the description we have often been told.

How can we be certain to become a part of the kingdom?
Just simply accept God and receive His perfect freedom.

No amount of good works will ever be justification,
God's love is gained only by salvation.

Sometimes a glimpse of heaven can be seen on earth,
By our many blessings bestowed to us after our rebirth.

Heaven is a divine place God has obtained for all,
If we will trust Him as our Savior and answer His call.

# DREAMS

The mystical magical realm of escape,
Where we all go to rest and meditate.
Dreams can be a pleasing journey to places unknown,
Often beginning as small children and continuing
when we are grown.

They can be visions of goals we hope to achieve,
But to realize them we must truly believe.
Dreams can be as clear as feeling fully awake,
Sometimes fearful and so overpowering
we can stir with a quake.

The mystical magical realm of escape,
Where we all go to rest and meditate.
Never give up on our dreams meant for success,
The power within will produce your best.

# MIRACLES

What exactly is this phenomenon known as a miracle?
Sometimes only obtainable by an act of faith and
high pinnacle.

Although many may say only coincidence,
Spirit-filled hearts know they are heavenly incidents.

A miracle can be seen in the smallest form,
But we must be sensitive to appreciate the not-so-norm.

Thousands of miracles happen time and time again,
Sadly, we often don't take notice to observe and comprehend.

If you will just trust and believe,
A seed of faith will allow a miracle to be received.

# A DESTINY WITH GOD

A power within calls me each day,
Drawing me closer than ever in the will of His way.

An awesome awareness that speaks gently to me,
Reminding me of His perfect example
I want to follow faithfully.

Daily guidance to witness and be a light
Of His love and become obedient in His sight.

Promises He has given are ours to redeem,
As long as we accept Jesus as our King.

A destiny with God is one given to me by grace
That insures when my time here is done, I will see His face.

Section 4

# FRIENDSHIP IS FOREVER

# THE SPIRIT OF FRIENDSHIP AND UNITY

The spirit of friendship and unity
Will bond us together in our community.

A ribbon and heart symbolizing hope
Will remind us of those struggling to cope.

Working together in our respective roles
Will strengthen us to accomplish our goals.

A genuine spirit of camaraderie and dedication
Will cement our dreams for harmony and unification.

May the spirit of friendship and unity
Tie us all together in love and loyalty.

# SPECIAL FRIENDSHIP

A special friendship is what we share,
One that is filled with trust and care.

A working relationship that flows smoothly every day
Because of the honesty and respect you always pay.

Little expressions of kindness shown each day,
Not due solely to obligation, but because of your special way.

A special friend I feel lucky to have found,
Unlike any other I have been around.

A chef, none to compare,
Is simply the best anywhere.

A special friendship I will always treasure,
A lasting bond I can never measure.

# SAYING GOODBYE

Saying goodbye is never an easy thing to do,
  Especially when it is conveyed to you.
  An Aide-de-Camp with a special flair,
Fulfilled your duties with the utmost care.

An important and valued part of the team,
You gave more than we ever imagined or dreamed.
  In one short year we came to rely
On your special talents that are hard to deny.

Saying goodbye to your special crew,
  Victoria, Bella, Clifford, and Joey too.
  We have been blest as so very few
Because we had the privilege to know you.

Saying goodbye now because you will depart
  Will fill us with sadness in our hearts.
We wish you the best in your future endeavors,
And please remember we will forget you never.

This is dedicated to my dear friend, Grace Rochelle,
who supported and lifted me while we were stationed
together at Fort Knox, Kentucky. Her husband, Major General Mike
Rochelle, and my husband commanded
at Fort Knox together and shared many common qualities.

# SAVING GRACE

Someone with a beautiful face
Became my friend and saving Grace.

Two women representing two major commands
Came together hoping to make a positive stand.

Brought together to fulfill a role,
We both strived to excel as our major goal.

Always ready to help anyway she could,
I was constantly aware of where she firmly stood.

If ever down or unable to decide,
I knew I had someone in whom I could confide.

Someone for whom I have the utmost admiration,
And I trust and owe special dedication.

Now we both will slow down the race,
But I will never forget my saving Grace.

"Divas" is dedicated to my dear friend Anita Craig.
We first met while our husbands were stationed in
Germany during the early 1970s. We have remained
closer than sisters ever since. This recognizes
thirty-nine years of faithful friendship.

# DIVAS

Divas are what we called each other,
As we traveled, shopped, and began to discover.
Two West Virginia girls who were newly Army wives,
Learning how to adjust and live the military life.

Divas are what we called each other,
As we traveled, shopped, and began to discover.
A chance meeting at a wives' tea
Would secure a lasting friendship since 1973.

Divas are what we called each other,
As we traveled, shopped, and began to discover.
Divas, although not known for any particular fame,
Would adopt this term just as our cutesy name.

Divas are what we called each other,
As we traveled, shopped, and began to discover.
The places and journeys we once made,
Left lasting memories that never will fade.

# A GIVING HEART IS
# THE DOOR TO FRIENDSHIP

A giving heart is the door to friendship,
One that beats true and extends kinship.
A new year to share and explore,
Welcoming all who enter our door.

A giving heart is the door to friendship,
One that beats true and extends kinship.
Working together at fundraising and events
Will build friendships that can't be bent.

A giving heart is the door to friendship,
One that beats true and extends kinship.
Giving hearts will see us through,
And build friendships that are forever true.

# GIRLFRIEND

A girlfriend like you is one of a kind,
For you are definitely a rare find.
Always there to brighten my day,
Knowing just the right words to convey.

Kindred spirits are we two,
So alike in all we do.
A girlfriend I rely on for help and advice,
One who always is genuinely nice.

And when I need a shoulder on which to cry,
I know you will forever be standing by.
No one could I ever trust more,
To be with, and wish the best for.

A girlfriend like you is one of a kind,
For you are definitely a rare find.
Whatever we do together, girlfriend,
Is a joy I hope will never end.

# FRIENDSHIP FOR ALL SEASONS

Sometimes we are lucky enough to find a friendship
for all seasons,
One that is placed in our lives for a time and special reason.

A friendship you always can depend on and trust,
Two qualities that are an absolute must.

Although it is rare to find that guiding light,
God's love will provide the star to shine in your darkest night.

Kindness, patience, and loyalty will forever insure
The gifts that will make a lasting friendship endure.

Always appreciate and never take for granted,
A chosen few who have stood by our sides, firmly planted.

A friendship for all seasons must be nurtured to stand the test
Of life's trials and joys and to share only the very best.

"A Fond Farewell to Our Chief" is dedicated to General Eric Shinseki, former Chief of Staff of the US Army, on the occasion of his retirement from the Army in 2003.

# A FOND FAREWELL
# TO OUR CHIEF

A fond farewell to our chief,
Your tenure has been much too brief.

Thanks for all your service of thirty-plus
And your commitment to defend and protect us.

It was right here at Fort Knox, Kentucky,
Your career began and made our nation lucky.

Your special "battle buddy" and wife
Has epitomized the military spouse's life.

We will long remember her grace
And her friendly, sincere face.

Our Chief, a soldier of honor, courage, and dedication,
One who holds our utmost admiration.

So farewell to our Chief Soldier,
We will miss your leadership and unfailing composure.

Section 5

# MILITARY ASSIGNMENTS AND FAMILIES

# I AM A MILITARY SPOUSE

I am a military spouse,
Always moving from house to house.
What it means to live this life
Is genuine pride and sometimes strife.

Traveling from east to west, and sometimes on foreign soil,
But always adjusting with moderate toil.
Coping with loneliness and separation,
Solely raising children with little vacation.

Learning acronyms and protocol,
Trying to be a master of all.
Lasting friendships sustained throughout the years
Will lovingly share our smiles and tears.

Although duty may call my spouse away,
On to remote battlefields in harm's way,
I will be vigilant and pray
For his safe return someday.

I am a military spouse,
Always moving from house to house.
Being a military spouse is a privilege and pleasure,
Filled with joy, honor, and memories to treasure.

# ALOHA, PARADISE

Willowy palm trees swaying in the breeze
Always filled my days with ease.
For every beautiful rainbow, waterfall, and sunset,
I will leave with tearful regret.

Craving the majestic views from Waianae,
the Ko'olaus, and Diamond Head,
Will leave me with an aching dread.
Remembering the somberness of Pearl and Punchbowl,
There will forever remain a stirring in my soul.

Island hopping to Maui, Molakai, and Kauai,
Will bring fond memories of Elvis and "My Blue Hawaii."
Enjoying each welcomed and refreshing Mauka shower,
Brings to mind the blossoms of every fragrant tropical flower.

Whether Bellows, Hickam, or Sunset Beach,
I will always treasure the crystal blue beauty of each.
Savory pineapple, coconut, macadamias, and shaved ice,
Are some of my favorite delights in paradise.

# ALOHA, PARADISE

Island shows such as Kealii Reichel, Legends,
and Society of Seven
Always managed to give me just a touch of heaven.
Reminiscences of luaus, ukuleles,
and steel guitars under the stars,
Accompanied by Chi Chis, Mai Tais,
or Blue Hawaiis at the bar.

It has been a joy to be part of the twenty-fifth team,
But now, much too soon, is the finale of this dream!
I will miss each one of you, so Mahalo and So Longa,
To all of you, my special Ohana.

God has blessed me and I have been so lucky,
But now I must bid aloha and leave for Kentucky!

# FAREWELL, FAITHFUL FRIENDS

Just as we were reuniting again,
Orders arrived and put our fun to an end.
Didn't have time to really play or explore,
Interrupted, while enjoying life at Fort Belvoir.

Although the good times were cut too short,
The treasured memories will linger on at our new fort.
Thanks for being such faithful friends,
The kind we can always trust, and on whom we can depend.

Even though miles may keep us far apart,
You are always close in our hearts.
Although now we must say farewell and depart,
Remember, faithful friends like us never really part.

# OUR TEAM

A group of players who all play
To win their objectives in an honorable way.

Inclusion and kindness set the tone,
So no one ever feels sad or alone.

Military families and civilians working together to achieve,
To set the standards for which we believe.

Building a team takes loyalty and trust,
Having solid principles is a must.

Just doing our best each and every day,
By giving a smile and stopping to pray.

Standing united will fulfill our small dream,
And make the Fort Knox players a special team.

# INSPIRING BY EXAMPLE

Inspiring by example are these very few
With their positive attitudes of "can do."

Whether volunteering in a school, helping a child to read,
Or helping coach sports, allowing them to succeed.

In a hospital, assisting with an emergency,
Or comforting a family with the utmost urgency.

Teaching Sunday school or joining a choir to sing,
With a talent that has a heavenly ring.

Sending a care package to "Any Soldier" just to show concern,
Hanging yellow ribbons on every tree,
anticipating a safe return.

Inspiring by example can be seen here every day,
By our Fort Knox volunteers who shine with
their winning ways.

# UNBRIDLED SPIRIT

Unbridled spirit is the feeling of pride,
One we want to emulate and not hide.

Just like a Kentucky thoroughbred running a race,
This is our goal to excel at a galloping pace.

A spirit that is welcoming and shows concern,
So everyone is treated respectfully in turn.

A new year to work and play together,
Building a team that will withstand any weather.

Our own Fort Knox Spouse's Club will strive to give our best,
With an unbridled spirit that outshines the rest.

# NEW HORIZONS

New horizons are now in view,
After losses that left me blue.

Friends and memories now left behind,
But new experiences and joys to find.

Losing a beloved pet that can never be replaced,
But finding comfort in the eyes of a new canine face.

Overwhelming bouts of heartbreak and grief,
Brought thoughts of denial and disbelief.

Valleys I have walked in sadness,
Now reveal God's power of happiness.

New horizons I can now face,
As I feel tranquility in God's chosen place.

# REMEMBERING AND
# REFLECTING

How swiftly twenty years have passed,
Since the 4th Squadron, 7th U.S. Cavalry moved fast.
From a small German town a deployment would commence,
Leaving families facing uncertainty and in suspense.

How swiftly twenty years have passed,
Since the 4th Squadron, 7th U.S. Cavalry moved fast.
Bradleys, choppers, and artillery all led the fight,
In a desert rage that would engage all night.

How swiftly twenty years have passed,
Since the 4th Squadron, 7th U.S. Cavalry moved fast.
Stopping a tyrant's brutality would undoubtedly cost
Brave comrades of Garry Owen to encounter significant loss.

Commemorating a time that will bond soldiers
and families forever,
Bringing back memories that will always keep them together.
How swiftly twenty years have passed,
Since the 4th Squadron, 7th U.S. Cavalry moved fast.

Section 6

# MY FAVORITE HOLIDAYS

# NEW YEAR'S WISHES

New Year's wishes being sent your way,
As we prepare to celebrate the year's first day.
From east to west celebrations will be seen,
As Father Time marches out in rapid stream.

The countdown will begin with noisemakers and light,
With champagne uncorking and a kiss at midnight.
As we ring in the New Year with "Auld Lang Syne,"
Thoughts of new resolutions will start to unwind.

New Year's wishes of health and happiness
Fill our hearts with the promise of gladness.
New Year's wishes being sent your way,
As we prepare to celebrate the year's first day.

# TIME FOR ROMANCE

A time for love and romance
Can be captured in a moment's glance.

Candlelight, music, and a moonlit night
Will help make the ambiance right.

A time when two hearts can share
All their dreams that prove they care.

Words spoken only through their eyes
Can send a signal that will hypnotize.

Anytime can be a time for romance,
A special occasion or a rendezvous by chance.

Take time for romance with the one you love,
For time shared together is a gift from above.

# CATCHING DERBY FEVER

Considered a holiday the first Saturday in May,
Is Kentucky's own renowned Derby Day.

The allure of horse racing can be found
At the famous track known as Churchill Downs.

Fashionable headwear decorated in bows, ribbons, and tulips,
Can be seen in the crowd with hands clutching cool mint
juleps.

Owners and trainers laying their bets down,
Hoping that their favorites will be crowned.

The Running for the Roses is the race to win,
Where each jockey and horse trail in a spin,

Considered a holiday the first Saturday in May,
Is Kentucky's own renowned Derby Day.

Only once a year will derby fever mount,
So enjoy each second and make it count.

# INDEPENDENCE DAY

A day all Americans should cherish and appreciate
Is one filled with parades and fireworks we excitedly celebrate.
We should thank God for our unique Independence Day,
And be on guard to ensure it is never taken away.

In 1776, our forefathers signed and guaranteed
our inalienable rights,
A nation built on principle, many have defended
with a continual fight.
We should thank God for our unique Independence Day,
And be on guard to ensure it is never taken away.

A flag that stands for justice and equality,
No other country can compare to its character and quality.
We should thank God for our unique Independence Day,
And be on guard to ensure it is never taken away.

Pride is the emotion that fills the night skies,
Each July 4th with beauty bursting before our eyes.
We should thank God for our unique Independence Day,
And be on guard to ensure it is never taken away.

# HALLOWEEN

Halloween is always a special October day,
Consisting of fun, costumes, and memories of yesterday.

Parades of characters crowd the street,
Going door to door to collect the best treats.

Vampires, witches, ghosts, and black cats
Can be seen at dusk amidst fog and flying bats.

A magical spell that is often cast just right,
As dancing and mischief light up the night.

One night to escape from reality and create a dream,
To become whatever we choose on this haunted
night we call Halloween.

# A TIME TO BE THANKFUL

A time to be thankful for the joys with which we're blest,
A time to pause, meditate, and to rest.

A time to give thanks to God above,
For family and friends who surround us with love.

Favorite traditions we observe in the fall,
Reflecting on memories of food, parades, and football.

A time to be mindful of those serving on the line,
So we can happily wine and dine.

Lest we forget the sacrifices they endure,
To make sure our freedom is insured.

A time to be thankful should occur each and every day,
To be grateful for a country where we can be free and pray.

# SIGHTS AND SOUNDS OF CHRISTMAS

Sights and sounds of Christmas are quickly
approaching again,
Where signs of the advent season are about to begin.

Symbols of the season can be found,
In Santa, reindeer, and toys all around.

Snow-covered trees, candlelight, and mistletoe,
Add a magical and special festive glow.

The hustle and bustle of shoppers in malls,
Children visiting Santa, baking, and decking the halls.

Familiar carols we all like to sing,
Paying respect to the living King.

The voices of an angelic choir,
Beckon us to be humble and admire.

May the sights and sounds of Christmas bring
you happiness and cheer,
And shine the light of joy, hope, and peace for the New Year.

## Section 7

# ELVIS THE KING

My passion for the life and times of Elvis Presley led me to write
"Long Live the King of Rock and Roll."

# LONG LIVE THE KING OF ROCK AND ROLL

Just a poor, humble country boy without
much to give him joy,
Having dreams of being a star, singing and
learning to play a guitar.
His Southern upbringing and dedication to his mother,
Gave him the perseverance to be better than any other.

Doing little that would bring him luck,
From minimal jobs and even driving a truck.
Then one day in a studio called "Sun",
A song called "That's All Right" would put him on the run.

An ex-carny man would give him a start,
Which allowed him to reach the top of the charts.
Recordings, TV, and movies all came,
And opened the door so he could achieve national fame.

Duty called and sent him away,
But he knew he would return someday.
After two years the fans were still true,
So he continued with his career and saw it though.

For awhile, marriage and a child would give him happiness,
But he couldn't rise above pressures of showbiz and duress.
More time on the road and concert dates,
Would finally lead him to meet his fate.

Just a poor, humble country boy,
Who would die alone on a bathroom floor.
Although he has left this world,
No one will ever forget the magic he unfurled.

So long live the King of Rock and Roll,
He will forever live in our souls.

"Legendary Soldier" was written on the occasion of the 46th anniversary of the day Elvis joined the Army.
Elvis was an Army Scout and served at Ft. Hood, Texas, and in Germany.

# LEGENDARY SOLDIER

A legendary soldier remembered by all,
Stood up and answered his nation's call.
A king, as he was known by his fans,
Now addressed as Private Presley, a military man.

An oath he took one March day,
To defend, protect, and diligently obey.
On the USS *Randall* he would set sail and depart,
Leaving behind tearful fans with broken hearts.

An Army Scout would be his military skill of success,
A Jeep driver with a special flair and finesse.
He always tried to do his very best,
Expecting to be treated like all the rest.

Skills he learned and lessons arousing his curiosity
Gave him the values and honor that demonstrated his
generosity.
A legendary soldier with an unforgettable face,
A patriot, entertainer, and star time cannot erase.

On September 26, 2008, Elvis Presley was honored
on the Las Vegas Walk of Stars. His star is in front of the Riviera Hotel,
where Elvis performed.
Our Viva Las Vegas Fan Club was instrumental
in raising funds for the star.
"A Star for Elvis" was written as a tribute for the dedication of his star.

# A STAR FOR ELVIS

Today a star will be unveiled,
In honor of an artist whose talents will forever prevail.

Liberace, Wayne Newton, and Sammy Davis,
a few of the names,
And now Elvis, the Las Vegas Walk of Stars may claim.

His mark on the strip was long-standing and great,
Bringing fans from all over the world to celebrate.

Viva Las Vegas fan clubbers diligently worked and fought,
To realize this dream to give Elvis his rightful spot.

May the star dedicated today always help to bring,
Special memories alive of our Rock and Roll king.